the bald eagle
returns

DOROTHY HINSHAW PATENT · WILLIAM MUÑOZ

the bald eagle returns

CLARION BOOKS
NEW YORK

THE AUTHOR AND PHOTOGRAPHER WISH TO THANK
RODGER KNAGGS, RILEY MCCLELLAND, BRIAN MEALEY, AND GRETA PARKS
FOR THEIR HELP WITH THIS BOOK.

This book is a revised, updated version of the author's and photographer's earlier book *Where the Bald Eagles Gather.*

FRONTISPIECE: *A bald eagle near St. Joseph, Missouri, surrounded by its snow geese prey.*

Clarion Books
a Houghton Mifflin Company imprint
215 Park Avenue South, New York, NY 10003
www.hmco.com/trade

Additional photograph credits:
NASA: p. 16
Chris Roberts: pp. 48, 51
Dorothy Hinshaw Patent: p. 56

The text was set in 15-point Meridien Roman.

Book design by Rachel Simon

Printed in Singapore.

Library of Congress Cataloging-in-Publication Data

Patent, Dorothy Hinshaw.
The bald eagle returns / by Dorothy Hinshaw Patent ; photographs by William Muñoz.
p.   cm.
Summary: Describes how bald eagles have recovered from the threat of extinction, how
they raise their families, and why they are important as the national bird of the United States.
ISBN 0-395-91416-7
1. Bald eagle—Juvenile literature. [1. Bald eagle. 2. Eagles.] I. Muñoz, William, ill. II. Title.

QL696.F32 P35 2000
598.9′43—dc21
00-021751

TWP 10 9 8 7 6 5 4 3 2 1

Dedicated to Brian, Greta, and all the other people
who work hard to help the bald eagle return
to its former range

contents

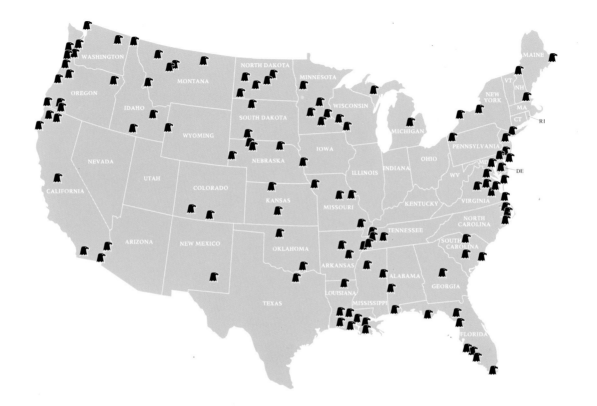

This map shows the approximate location of National Wildlife Refuges where bald eagles live. Contact the U.S. Fish and Wildlife Service, Department of the Interior, for exact locations to visit. The Web site *www.baldeagleinfo.com* is also a good resource for the best places to see bald eagles, including National Wildlife Refuges.

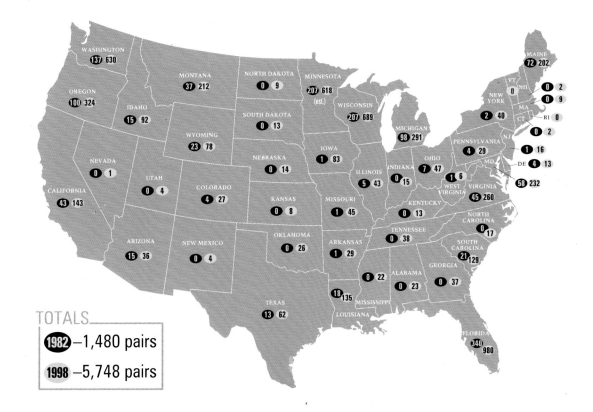

TOTALS

1982 –1,480 pairs

1998 –5,748 pairs

This map shows how the number of nesting pairs of bald eagles has increased in the lower forty-eight states between 1982 and 1998. The figures on the left are the number of nesting pairs in 1982; the figures on the right indicate the number of pairs in 1998. Bald eagles have always been numerous in Alaska; there are no bald eagles in Hawaii.

People once came to Apgar Bridge in Glacier National Park, Montana, to see bald eagles every fall.

When our book *Where the Bald Eagles Gather* was published in 1984, the bald eagle was in trouble. Throughout the lower forty-eight states, only 1,757 pairs of eagles nested. In most of the country, our national symbol was endangered, threatened with extinction.

Today, approximately six thousand pairs of bald eagles raise their families throughout the United States, many in places that haven't seen them for decades. A tale of peril has turned into a story of success. In this book, you will find out how these magnificent birds have returned to their ancient homes across America. You will discover how they raise their families and also learn about their importance as the national bird of the United States.

With its more than seven-foot wingspan, a bald eagle is an impressive sight when it soars through the air.

the bald eagle soared over the brown winter meadow. Its yellow eyes spotted a ripple in the grass. The bird tilted its tail and banked slowly to the left. For a second it paused in the air, then plunged downward, spreading its powerful, sharp talons just as it reached the unsuspecting jackrabbit. The eagle struck the rabbit and tightened its grip with its talons. Then the hungry bird lifted its catch slowly from the ground and flew to a nearby tree to feed.

With its shining white head and tail and its brownish black body, the powerful adult bald eagle cannot be mistaken for any other bird. It is one of America's largest birds. Its body is up to 3 feet (.9 m) long, and its wings can spread from 7 feet to almost 8 feet (2 to 2.1 m). Female bald eagles tend to be larger than males.

The golden eagle also lives in America. The adult golden eagle looks very different from the bald eagle. It is dark brown, with light

The light feathers on the back of a golden eagle's head inspired its name.

reddish brown feathers on its neck that gleam golden in the sun. Young golden eagles usually have some white on the wings and a white tail with a dark band at its tip. It is not always easy to tell a young golden eagle from a young bald eagle. Both are dark brown with white on the underside of the wings and tail. The immature bald eagle can have white on other parts of its body and is more mottled in appearance. The bald eagle's beak turns yellow as it grows older, while the tip of the golden eagle's beak is always dark. When

LEFT: *An adult golden eagle*

An immature bald eagle often has white feathers mixed in with brown ones. Notice that the lower legs are free of feathers. The lower legs of golden eagles are covered by feathers.

the birds are perched, you may be able to see that the feathers of a golden eagle cover its legs all the way to the tops of its feet.

The two American eagles eat different food. Golden eagles hunt rabbits and large rodents like ground squirrels and prairie dogs. Bald eagles feed mostly on fish. They also eat birds, especially ones that live around water, such as snow geese. Some bald eagles feed heavily on jackrabbits during the winter.

The bald eagle is perfectly adapted for the hunting life. Its feet are equipped with sharp, curved talons 1½ inches (3.8 cm) long for grasping prey. Tiny spikes on the bottoms of its toes help grip slippery fish. Its powerful hooked beak, which is used to tear food apart, is 2 inches (5 cm) long.

Eagles, along with their close relatives the hawks, have very sharp vision. They can see a small animal, such as a rabbit or even a mouse, moving in the grass from a mile away. Most animals have one especially sensitive spot on the retina of the eye called the fovea, where images are magnified and sharply focused. An eagle's fovea has about five times as many light-sensitive cells as that of a human,

The eyes of eagles, as you can see with this young bird, face forward.

so it can see things in much finer detail. Also, an eagle has two foveas in each eye instead of one. One fovea improves vision to the side, while the other heightens forward vision.

Hawks and eagles have eyes that face forward, like ours. Each eye has a slightly different field of vision, which gives the bird good depth perception. Like us, it can judge distances very well. This is important to a hunter, who must know just when to pounce on its prey.

Successful hunting requires perfect timing. A hungry bald eagle perches on a tree by the water's edge or soars over the surface in

The eagle's talons are powerful weapons for seizing prey.

search of fish. When it spots prey, it flies over the spot. For a moment, the bird is suspended in the air, wings spread out. Then it tilts its tail and dives. As the eagle whizzes close to the fish, it flings its toes forward with outstretched talons. At the last moment, it reaches through the water and grabs the fish, tightening its grasp, piercing its prey with sharp talons. The talons lock onto the fish so that it cannot struggle free. Then the eagle flies to a nearby perch to feast. It holds its prey with its talons while it tears off bites of food with its powerful pointed beak.

A bald eagle needs up to a pound (.5 kg) of food each day to maintain its weight. With its strong wings, it can lift a load weighing up to 3 pounds (1.4 kg). It isn't choosy about what it eats. A bald eagle is just as content with a dead fish or bird as a live one. Bald eagles are not above stealing, either. If an eagle sees an osprey with a fish, it may well attack the smaller bird, forcing it to give up its prey.

Bald eagles, especially young birds that haven't perfected their hunting skills, often feed on road-killed deer. This can create a problem. When an eagle has gorged itself on meat, its body is heavy,

Eagles are often injured by cars, trains, or electric wires. This golden eagle is lucky; it is well enough to return to the wild, as Sean Muñoz, the photographer's son, and wildlife rehabilitator Kate Davis look on.

so it needs to fly quite a distance to get up enough speed to gain altitude. A straight, flat road makes the best runway. But as the bird flies down the road, it can crash into an approaching car and be seriously injured or even killed. Wildlife rehabilitators can sometimes nurse wounded eagles back to health, but often these birds never recover enough to be released into the wild again.

Like most birds, eagles are designed for flight. The heavier an object is, the more energy it takes for it to become and remain airborne, so birds need to be lightweight. Birds have hollow bones, and their feathers weigh very little. Despite its impressive size, a bald eagle weighs only 8 to 14 pounds (3.6 to 6.4 kg), with birds in Alaska being the heaviest.

The wings of different birds are designed to suit their way of life. Birds like swallows are made for quick turns and twists in rapid flight. Their wings are pointed and narrow. Eagles are made for soaring on the wind. They need to be able to stay in the air, looking for food, without wasting energy flapping their wings. An eagle has broad, strong wing feathers that provide a lot of surface area. Because of this, it can be carried by updrafts and sail over the land like a hang glider. The spread-out tail feathers also help keep the eagle airborne. The eagle maneuvers in the air and lands through movements of its flight and tail feathers.

A bird's feathers get broken from wear and tear, and need to be replaced. Some birds lose most of their feathers over a short time and cannot fly while the new ones are growing in. But eagles always need to be able to fly, since they hunt on the wing. They lose only a few feathers at a time. Some of an eagle's flight feathers can last for two or even three years.

The smooth surface feathers on a bird's body help it slip through the air as it flies. Birds also have fluffy feathers close to their bodies that hold in body warmth. Most birds, including eagles, have an oil gland near the base of the tail. They use their beaks to spread the oil over their feathers to protect them from becoming waterlogged. The oil prevents the feathers from getting wet when an eagle hunts fish.

The eagle tips its fan of tail feathers to help it turn.

bald eagles mate for life and return to the same area each spring. The birds use the same nest year after year, repairing it when necessary, for the giant structures take a long time to build. If one bird dies, however, the survivor will try to find a new mate. Eagle nests may also be occupied by different birds over the years. One nest in Ohio was used over and over for thirty-six years.

The bald eagle's nest is made of sticks of dead wood lined with grass, feathers, moss, pine needles, or other soft materials. It can be 8 to 9 feet (2.4 to 2.7 m) wide, 20 feet (6 m) deep, and weigh as much as 2 tons. The nest must be large enough to withstand wind and weather and to serve as an exercise platform for the young birds when they are old enough to learn to fly.

Old tall trees near water are the favorite location for bald eagles to

OPPOSITE: *Bald eagles like to build their nests high in trees, where they have a good view of their surroundings.*

Both parents defend the nest if they feel threatened, rushing out and calling at the intruder. Their voices are high and sound similar to those of gulls. Sometimes they even attack.

This chick is losing its second set of down feathers as its juvenile feathers grow in.

nest. However, in the treeless far north, nests are built on the edges of cliffs or on grassy knolls. In the Southwest desert, bald eagles have been found nesting on cliffs and on top of large cactuses.

The female eagle lays one, two, or three (usually two) dull white eggs, one to three days apart. In Florida, the eggs are laid during the winter, but over most of the bald eagle's range, family life begins in the early spring. The parents take turns incubating the eggs, but the female usually spends more time on the nest than the male. Besides keeping the eggs warm, the parents protect them from squirrels, ravens, and gulls, which might eat them. The eggs hatch in about

TOP: *One chick has just hatched in this eagle nest at the Kennedy Space Center in Florida. This and the following NASA photos were taken by a remote-control camera installed near the nest. Notice the other egg that has yet to hatch.* BOTTOM LEFT: *The parent bird feeds its chick very gently.* BOTTOM RIGHT: *One of the chicks tries out its wings as a parent watches.*

five weeks. The hatchlings are covered with soft, fluffy light gray feathers. When the chicks are about three weeks old, they lose their hatchling feathers as a thicker coat of darker gray feathers grows in. These feathers remain until the juvenile feathers, which will enable them to fly, grow in.

At first, the male eagle does most of the hunting for the family while the female guards the small chicks. As the youngsters grow bigger and stronger, she takes on more of the hunting duties. The parents feed the young chicks by tearing off small bits of food and gently holding them in their beaks for the youngsters to take.

The chicks grow fast, gaining about a pound (.5 kg) a week. By the time they are four weeks old, they can stand and are able to tear off their own mouthfuls of food from carcasses the parents deposit in the nest. By six weeks, they are almost as big as their parents, and their black juvenile feathers are coming in fast. When food is abundant, both chicks get enough to eat. But if food is scarce, the larger chick, which hatched first, will be the only one to survive.

Eight-week-old chicks begin to develop their flight muscles by standing on the nest and beating their wings. Sometimes their feet leave the nest, but they are not ready to fly yet. Between ten and thirteen weeks, the youngsters are ready to spread their wings and fly. The parents circle nearby, calling loudly, and they may tempt their young into flying by swooping by them while carrying food. The eaglets finally leave the nest. At first, they fly only short distances, landing clumsily on nearby branches or on the ground.

For the next few weeks, the young birds stay close to the nest. They still depend on their parents for food. They continue to practice flying as their flight muscles gain in strength, and they become more and more graceful both in flight and when landing. They are learning how to survive on their own.

It takes a long time to become a successful hunter. As winter approaches, the parents and eaglets separate. Most bald eagles migrate to warmer climates in the fall and come back to their nesting areas in the spring. Eagles living in the north fly south, looking for food as waters freeze over. The young eagles do best when they find streams with spawning salmon. After laying their eggs, the salmon

This young bald eagle just finished its first flight and ended up landing on a stump.

Here, a young eagle gets a meal by snagging a dead salmon and dragging it back to shore.

die, and all a young bird has to do to get a meal is wade out into the water and snag a fish with its talons. The first winter is the most difficult time of life for a young eagle. If it can survive the test of learning to hunt for itself, it may live to be twenty-five to thirty years old.

The young bald eagle's eyes and beak are brown at first. As the bird grows older, both the beak and the eyes get lighter, slowly turning yellow. The black juvenile feathers are gradually replaced by dark brown ones, along with some white feathers. By the time the eagle is four to five years old, the brilliant white head and tail feathers of the adult grow in.

Scientists in Glacier National Park measure a young bald eagle.

Until the mid-1980s, bald eagles gathered every fall along McDonald Creek in Glacier National Park to feast on the kokanee salmon that swam up from Flathead Lake to spawn. This annual event attracted thousands of people, who came to watch hundreds of eagles swooping down to snag salmon and resting in trees along the creek.

Then the salmon population collapsed, and the great gathering of eagles ended. What had happened?

In the 1980s, a small animal called the opossum shrimp was introduced into Flathead Lake as food for the young salmon. Unfortunately, the shrimp competed with the fish for food instead of serving as meals for them. They were very efficient at eating the tiny water fleas that are the principle food for the very young salmon,

23

and the salmon disappeared. All efforts to restore the salmon to the lake have failed because the opossum shrimp cannot be removed.

During the 1970s and 1980s, scientists captured some of the eagles in Glacier National Park. They took many measurements of the birds. One of the few ways to tell if a bird is a male or a female is to measure its beak, for females have bigger beaks than males. The eagles were weighed and their wingspans measured. The scientists also felt along the breastbone to see how fat the birds were.

The eagles were fitted with numbered plastic wing markers that were brightly colored so they could be easily seen. Each year, a different color was used, and other colors were used to mark birds from other places in North America where eagles gathered. That way, someone could tell from a distance both the year and the place where the bird had been tagged.

A few birds were also equipped with small, lightweight radio transmitters. The transmitter was fastened to the bird's tail. The wire antenna of each transmitter was carefully tied and glued along the tail feathers. It hung a few inches beyond the tail. The birds acted as

The bright wing markers with large numbers are easy to read.

The antenna of the radio transmitter is tied into the bird's tail feathers.

if the antenna was just a very long feather, preening it as if it belonged.

Each transmitter put out a unique signal, so each bird could be tracked with a radio receiver. This allowed the scientists to follow the bird and see where it went after leaving the park.

A special receiver was used to locate the birds with transmitters. The receiver could be carried along the ground or taken up in an airplane. The scientists could adjust the receiver to pick up the frequencies of different birds. When the receiver picked up a signal, the tracker would hear beeping through a set of earphones. The closer to the eagle, the louder the sound. Using the receiver, a scientist could track the eagle to its exact location.

By tracking the eagles, scientists learned that although a few of the birds spent the winter in western Montana, most kept moving south. Many made their winter homes in the Rush Valley in Utah. Here, a hundred eagles might roost together at night in a single stand of cottonwood trees, feeding by day on jackrabbits, which were abundant in the area. Other birds, such as hawks and crows, joined the eagles in the trees. A few of the Glacier Park eagles traveled farther south or west. Some ended up in Oregon, while others journeyed as far as the Nevada edge of California. This is 750 miles (1200 km) from Glacier Park.

The tagged birds were also followed all the way to their nesting areas in the spring. In March, the eagles began their northerly migration. The adult birds hurried to reach their summer homes and start their families, so they moved steadily northward. They flew as far as 200 miles (320 km) a day and usually didn't stop in one place for very long. Young birds, unconcerned about family life, took longer.

The eagles traveled north past Glacier National Park, flying on the eastern side of the Rocky Mountains. On and on they went, through the Canadian province of Alberta, all the way to the shores of Great Bear Lake and Great Slave Lake in the Northwest Territories. Here the birds stopped, the adults meeting up with their mates to raise families. Although these eagles no longer visit Glacier Park to feed on salmon, they still follow much the same migration route year after year.

Alaskan eagles that live inland tend to migrate to the coast, where the seawater remains unfrozen for the winter. Some

An eagle and two ravens wait to feed on a road-killed deer.

British Columbia eagles do not migrate, while others fly down the coast into Washington and Oregon.

Eagles taggged in eastern North America also were found to migrate. Those that breed in northern Canada migrate into southern Canada and New England. Birds that raise their families in the Middle Atlantic states spend the winter in Georgia and northern Florida. Bald eagles that live in Florida migrate only short distances within the state or stay put.

An eagle is alert to danger near its nest in the Florida Keys.

Scientists continue to study bald eagles. Some use the time-honored methods of tagging and tracking. Others use newer methods. Since 1992, Brian Mealey, a wildlife biologist at the Miami Museum of Science, in partnership with Everglades National Park, has been studying the blood chemistry of eaglets. Almost twenty pairs of bald eagles nest on the small islands in Florida Bay, an estuary of Everglades National Park. Mealey and his colleagues take blood samples from young eagles before they leave the nest. They also band the young birds. Like the Glacier birds, each one has its own band, so it can be identified if it is injured or killed.

Back at their laboratory at the Falcon Batchelor Bird of Prey Center, they measure the amounts of certain chemicals in the eaglets' blood. A lot can be learned about the health of an animal by looking at its blood chemistry. But first, normal values for the various chemicals need to be known. Mealey hopes to determine the normal values and discover whether the eagles are in danger of health problems now.

Blood samples can help show if the birds suffer from toxins,

LEFT: *Greta Parks and Brian Mealey band a young bald eagle.*
RIGHT: *Mealey transfers an eagle blood sample to a vial to take to the laboratory.*

parasites, or any other ailments. They can also help determine if the birds are getting enough food and water. With all the data currently being collected, scientists in the future will be able to tell much about the normal health of bald eagles. They will then be able to discover health problems at an early stage and develop proper procedures for treating them or eliminating their causes.

Scenes like this, with many eagles in one place, were common before European settlement of North America.

No one knows how many bald eagles lived in North America before European settlement. But once bald eagles could be seen in every state except Hawaii. Estimates of the numbers in what now are the lower forty-eight states run from 25,000 to 75,000 or even more. These numbers decreased slowly as more and more people moved across the continent, cutting down forests and building cities along the shores where bald eagles once lived.

For the first 350 years after white settlement began, the numbers of bald eagles probably dropped steadily as their habitat disappeared. In the middle of the nineteenth century, people living on Manhattan Island in New York City could watch bald eagles fish in the Hudson River and carry their prey into Central Park to feast. As recently as 1890, bald eagles nested all along the shores of Chesapeake Bay, with at least one nest per mile (1.6 km).

four • decline of the eagle

Eagles must have peace and quiet in order to raise their families. Bald eagles will nest on cliffs if there are no trees available, but normally they require big trees to support their heavy nests. The old-growth forests, where such trees are found, have unfortunately been a favorite source of timber, giving way everywhere to the saw.

During the late 1940s, bald eagle populations began to drop alarmingly. And where the eagles survived, few bred successfully. They disappeared rapidly from area after area, state after state. By the mid-1960s, many biologists feared that our national bird would disappear forever. Fewer than five hundred breeding pairs of bald eagles were left in the lower forty-eight states.

Luckily, scientists soon discovered the major cause—the pesticide DDT. Starting in the late 1940s, DDT was widely used to control such insects as mosquitoes and crop pests. DDT got into the food chain, and eagles ate contaminated fish and other prey. The pesticide didn't kill the birds, but it caused the shells of their eggs to be thinner and weaker. When the parent nestled up to the eggs to warm them, the shells would break, killing the developing bird inside.

OPPOSITE: *Bald eagles usually prefer peaceful sites away from noise and people to build their nests.*

Like the eagle, the osprey population was devastated by DDT. Now this great fish-eating bird is making a comeback. This bird is carrying a stick to add to its nest.

Eagles weren't the only victims. Hawks, peregrine falcons, ospreys, pelicans, and other birds were also disappearing. Evidence kept piling up that DDT was to blame.

Although DDT was banned in the United States in 1972, eagles still face other dangers. Pollutants in the environment, such as PCBs and dieldrin, can also harm them. Sometimes a chemical is used for a long time before we find out it endangers wildlife. Then, even if it is banned, it lingers in the environment and can continue to cause problems for years to come.

Eagles also die from other human activities. They are frequently electrocuted by power lines. However, many electric companies now work with scientists to make power lines and poles safe for eagles and other large birds.

Some people kill eagles for their feathers. Indians use eagle feathers for their traditional ceremonies. Non-Indians also value eagle feathers and may be willing to pay a lot of money for them. But no one can legally kill eagles to get their feathers. A single eagle feather is worth as much as seventy-five dollars, while a tail fan can sell for four hundred dollars on the illegal market. These high prices attract some people to areas where eagles gather in large numbers, to kill the birds illegally for profit.

And in states where animals are trapped for furs, eagles may be attracted to the bait in a trap and get caught. Because eagles hunt by sight, they are attracted only to the bait of traps set in the open. In many states, traps must be placed out of sight so that eagles will not find them. But if traps are put where they can be seen, eagles can be hurt. When a steel trap snaps shut on an eagle's foot, it can cut the skin and break bones. Injured birds' feet take a long time to heal. Because eagles use their feet to capture their food, an injured bird can starve to death before its foot heals.

Lead shot from guns used to hunt ducks and geese also killed bald eagles. Wounded birds or ones hunters failed to retrieve became eagle food, and the lead shot in the birds' bodies poisoned the eagles. A five-year program that phased out the use of lead shot began in 1986, benefiting many kinds of birds, including eagles.

Unfortunately, many people have mistaken ideas about eagles and think that they are harmful animals. Both bald eagles and golden eagles may feed on dead animals killed by other causes. And occasionally, golden eagles kill young lambs. For these reasons, many ranchers believe that all eagles are a serious danger to their livestock. Some ranchers hate eagles enough to shoot them, even though it is against the law.

This eagle nest has been built in a perfect habitat—a tall tree near water and away from human interference.

In 1973, the Endangered Species Act (ESA) was passed by Congress. This vital piece of legislation protects plants and animals whose populations are so small that they are in danger of disappearing forever—of becoming extinct. The bald eagle already had some protection from earlier laws, but it was one of the first species to be protected under the ESA.

The ESA has two categories: "endangered" and "threatened." An endangered species has reached the point where it could easily disappear unless it receives protection and help in recovering. A threatened species needs protection so that it doesn't reach the level of being endangered. The bald eagle was declared endangered in forty-three of the lower forty-eight states. In the other five states—Michigan, Minnesota, Oregon, Washington, and Wisconsin—it was labeled as threatened.

When a species is listed as endangered, a Species Survival Plan is developed to help increase its numbers. To be successful, the plan must deal with the problems the species faces. Just like people, animals need homes in order to live successfully and raise families. Besides big trees for their nests, bald eagles need clean waterways with abundant fish and birds to provide food.

Protecting eagle habitat has been a very important part of the recovery effort. Cutting large old trees in eagle country was discouraged. When eagles chose to nest on public land, the birds' status as an endangered species meant that people were restricted from the area to avoid disturbing the birds.

The eagles also need to be protected from humans who might harm them. Killing an endangered animal is against the law, and the penalties can be expensive. For example, an Oregon rancher once made the mistake of shooting an eagle that had been tagged with orange wing markers and a radio transmitter in Glacier National Park. He removed the markers but missed the transmitter under her tail. The young bird, nicknamed Patience, had flown more than

LEFT: *Biologists use a mirror on the end of a long pole to see if an eagle nest contains eggs.*
RIGHT: *The mirror clearly shows that there is an egg in this nest.*

500 miles (800 km) from Glacier and had been tracked all along the way. When the radio signal from her transmitter stopped moving, scientists traced it to a rubbish heap on the rancher's land. He confessed to shooting the bird, thinking she was a danger to his livestock. He was fined $2,500 for his crime, which had resulted in the loss of a valuable source of information on bald eagle movements as well as the death of a healthy young eagle. When people know they can face hefty fines for killing endangered animals, they will think twice before shooting.

By 1974, the ban on DDT had started to have beneficial effects, and nearly eight hundred bald eagle pairs were trying to raise families in the lower forty-eight states. This was a hopeful beginning for the return of the bald eagle.

The scientists in charge of bald eagle recovery also wanted to help the eagles increase their numbers by raising chicks in captivity. Captive eagles were sent to the Patuxent Wildlife Research Center in Maryland and bred there. As soon as the female eagle in each pair had laid her first clutch of eggs, the eggs were removed and incubated artificially. Most females went on to lay another clutch, which the parents were allowed to incubate. In this way, four eaglets instead of two could be raised from each mated pair. By the time the program ended in 1988, 124 bald eagles had been hatched for release into the wild.

Young eagles can learn to live on their own through a method called hacking. When the eaglets are eight weeks old, they are given a new home in a cage that's placed high on a tower in the wild. The site is one where few, if any, bald eagles live but one that provides good habitat. Humans, who stay out of sight, bring food to the young birds. When the eagles are twelve weeks old, the cage is removed so they can leave when ready to fly. Food is left for them until they can hunt well enough to feed themselves.

Another way to raise eaglets is to remove the third egg, or a young eaglet from a large clutch, and place it in the nest of a pair whose eggs didn't hatch. The foster parents then raise the chick as their own.

The efforts to save bald eagles have paid off. The number of breeding pairs in the lower forty-eight states has steadily increased until it reached almost 4,500 pairs in 1995. The U.S. Fish and Wildlife Service announced in July 1995 that the bald eagle was out of immediate danger of extinction and therefore no longer endangered. It reclassified the birds as threatened throughout the lower forty-eight.

In 1998, it was estimated that 5,748 pairs of bald eagles were nesting in the lower forty-eight, with pairs in every state except Rhode Island and Vermont. Federal officials felt that the bald eagle had safely recovered and could continue to thrive without special protection. They proposed removing the bald eagle completely from the list of endangered species in 2000. Other regulations outside the Endangered Species Act offer enough protection for our national bird, they believe.

Many scientists and other friends of the bald eagle disagree. They fear that if it is not carefully protected, eagle habitat will be lost, along with the eagles that depend upon it.

A pair of bald eagles call to each other.

Darcy Anaquod, a young dancer from the Anishanabe tribe in Canada, wears a traditional costume with young golden eagle feathers in a visor, part of the headdress. The visor contains twelve tail feathers, the same number as in an eagle's tail.

humans have looked to nature for meaning since the beginning of recorded time. Large and beautiful predators such as eagles have been valued around the world as symbols of power and freedom. In 3500 B.C., the Sumerians, who lived in the Euphrates River valley in what is now Iraq, believed that eagles carried men's souls to heaven. To the ancient Greeks, the eagle was a symbol of Zeus, the ruler of the heavens. The Aztecs founded their great city of Tenochtitlán at the place where they saw an eagle perched on a cactus. The small temple they built there evolved into the Great Pyramid of Tenochtitlán, which lies in the heart of modern Mexico City.

Both golden eagles and bald eagles hold a special place in the spirituality of Native Americans in North America. Eagle feathers were and are considered very powerful, for they embody the qualities of the great eagle itself. Eagles are symbols of peace, and the birds can serve as messengers between people and the Creator. Their feathers can carry prayers. The hollow bones of eagle wings were once used by medicine men to draw away disease.

If an eagle was killed, its spirit was honored by special ceremonies and prayers. In order to obtain eagle feathers without killing the birds, Native Americans built stone structures on hilltops for capturing eagles. Bait was placed there, and a young man would wait, hidden in the structure below, until an eagle landed. At just the right moment, the Indian would grab the eagle's legs and pluck its feathers, then release the bird. Obtaining feathers in this way was an act of bravery acknowledged by the tribe.

Today, only Native Americans are allowed by law to possess eagle feathers. They must apply to the government to obtain them. The U.S. Fish and Wildlife Service holds the feathers in its National Eagle Repository in Denver. From there, eagle claws, single feathers, wings, and tail fans are sent to tribal members around the country whose

This traditional bustle from the Schemitzun Bustle Center in Hartford, Connecticut, is made from bald eagle tail feathers.

applications have been approved. The birds used are victims of road kills, electrocutions, illness, and other misfortunes.

The Founding Fathers of the United States chose the bald eagle as the national bird. They viewed it as a symbol of freedom and placed it on the Great Seal of the United States in 1782. Not everyone agreed with the choice, however. Benjamin Franklin gave his opinion of the bald eagle in a letter to his daughter in 1784:

I wish the Bald Eagle had not been chosen as the Representative of our Country. He is a Bird of bad moral Character. He does not get his Living honestly. You may have seen him perch'd on some dead Tree near the River, where, too lazy to fish for himself, he watches the Labour of the Fishing Hawk [osprey] and, when that diligent Bird has at length taken a Fish, and is bearing it to his Nest for the Support of his Mate and young Ones, the bald Eagle pursues him and takes it from him. With all this Injustice, he is never in good Case but like those among Men who live by Sharping and Robbing he is generally poor and often very lousy. Besides, he is a rank Coward: The little King Bird *no bigger than a Sparrow attacks him boldly and drives him out of the District.*

Most Americans, however, did and still do love this beautiful, powerful bird. Besides the Great Seal, the bald eagle appears on the emblems of twelve states and is used as the symbol of many companies and organizations across the country.

Descriptions of animals as being bad or good because of their way of life were once commonly made, even by naturalists like

Eagle Scout pin

John James Audubon, who agreed with Franklin about the character of the bald eagle. Today, scientists and many others understand that it makes no sense to judge animals as we would people. Each species has its place, and every living thing has its own right to exist.

Humans can help or harm other forms of life. When we cut down a forest, we kill plants and animals as well as trees. When we build a dam, we destroy the homes of many kinds of life. On the other hand, when we set aside a wilderness area, we protect the plants and animals that live there. It is important for us to understand the power we have over living things and to use that power wisely.

A bald eagle flies in Glacier National Park in the fall.

Alaska is home to thousands of bald eagles, such as these young birds.

many areas of the United States now offer the opportunity to see bald eagles. If you go eagle watching, remember that these birds prefer to live near water, where the fish and waterfowl they eat most often live. If you spot an eagle nest, be sure to keep your distance and be very quiet, so as not to disturb the family. And remember, the place you're most likely to see an eagle is straight up over your head, soaring on the wind.

If you are going to travel to see eagles, it's a good idea to check with national and state parks and with local chapters of the National Audubon Society to learn about the best viewing opportunities. National Wildlife Refuges are often good places to see bald eagles.

Even though the population of bald eagles in Alaska has had its ups and downs, large numbers have always lived there. Today, scientists believe Alaska holds as many bald eagles as the habitat will

seven • where the bald eagles gather today

support. Alaska and the Canadian province of British Columbia are probably home to fifty thousand or so bald eagles. During the winter, the largest gathering of these birds on the continent descends on the Chilkat River in Alaska. Thousands gather there to feed on a very late run of spawning chum and sockeye salmon. The nearby town of Haines holds an annual eagle festival to celebrate the gathering. People come from all over to see the show.

Alaska is a long way to travel for most people. But now that the bald eagle continues to increase its population in the lower forty-eight states, more and more people will be lucky enough to see this magnificent bird. Only a few years ago, bald eagles were rare in New York. But today, a few can be seen along the Hudson River.

Thanks to a hacking site set up in 1976 and used until 1980, the bald eagle has returned successfully to Montezuma National Wildlife Refuge in central New York State, near Seneca Falls. More than 130,000 people visit the refuge each year to see eagles and many other kinds of birds, especially those that live on and around water, such as egrets and geese.

A bald eagle in Florida

Florida has more nesting bald eagles than any other state in the lower forty-eight. In 1998, 980 pairs were counted there. January through April is the nesting season in Florida, and these months provide the best opportunity to view eagles as they hunt food for their rapidly growing brood.

Hawk Mountain Sanctuary in eastern Pennsylvania is a popular

Many bald eagles feed during the winter in northwestern Nebraska. Here, an adult bald eagle decides to chase a young one away from its feeding area.

place to view migrating birds. From August 15 to December 15, around eighteen thousand hawks, falcons, and eagles of sixteen species pass by the sanctuary's lookout. In 1998, that included 154 bald eagles.

Wisconsin and Minnesota both have more than six hundred nesting pairs of bald eagles, which can be seen along the shores of lakes and rivers. In Minnesota, the Chippewa National Forest is home to more than 330 breeding pairs. Many of the lakes in the forest feature a giant eagle nest in a tree along the shore, making the forest a perfect place to see eagles during the spring and summer.

During the winter, bald eagles gather at several sites along the Missouri and Mississippi Rivers. Near St. Joseph, Missouri, about three hundred eagles gather to feed on migrating snow geese from mid-November to the middle of December. In other places along these big rivers, the flow of water through dams helps keep some of the water free of ice all winter. In addition, the turbines that generate electricity injure and kill many fish, providing easy meals for eagles. Even young birds that haven't yet learned how to hunt can find plenty of food.

Bald eagles can also be seen along the West Coast. Washington State is home to almost six hundred active eagle nests. In January, chum salmon gather in the Skagit River to breed. More than 450 eagles join them, feeding on the salmon that die after spawning.

In southern Oregon, near the California border, about three hundred bald eagles roost in the winter in Bear Valley National Wildlife Refuge. The refuge is closed to visitors during the winter, but the eagles fly out every morning to feed on the ducks and geese that winter in the Klamath River basin, especially on sick or injured birds.

Many of the birds that once gathered in Glacier National Park now find food near Helena, Montana, in the fall. Below Canyon Ferry Dam on the Missouri River, about three hundred birds feed on kokanee salmon, just as they once did in Glacier. The salmon spawn from mid-October until early December.

We can hope that our national bird will continue to grow in

An eagle heads off to fish below Canyon Ferry Dam on the Missouri River in Montana.

The return of the bald eagle is something to celebrate.

number as the years go by. So much of America is now taken over by human activity that we will never see the tens of thousands of eagles that once lived here. But perhaps someday every American can have the thrill of seeing a bald eagle soaring high on the wind overhead.

Page numbers in **bold** refer to illustrations.

index